Darkness Lies Forever In The Heart

A Volume of Poetry

Joshua Pavelsky

Copyright ©2024 Joshua Pavelsky
Publisher Fae Corps LLC

All rights reserved. This book or any portion thereof may not be reproduced or used in any manner whatsoever without the express written permission of the publisher except for the use of brief quotations in a book review.

Fae Corps LLC
5415 Raven Dr
Charleston WV 25 306
Faecorpspublishing.com

Editor & Cover art: Patricia Harris

Dedicated To
Heather Walters
Aaliyah Tillman
Steven Pavelsky

In the shadows of my mind, a darkness weaves,
A whispering void where memory grieves,
Faint echoes of light, now shadows drawn,
In corners where hope and joy have gone.

Silent specters, with secrets to keep,
Lurk in the places where shadows sleep,
A tangle of thoughts, a web of despair,
Threads of the night, spun in the air.

Eyes closed, I see them, dancing in gloom,
Ghosts of my fears in a shadowed room,
They murmur of past, of pain untold,
Of dreams that wither, of hearts grown cold.

Yet in this dark, a flicker remains,
A stubborn ember through sorrow's reins,
A spark of defiance, a whisper of dawn,
In the heart of shadows, where light is drawn.

For even in darkness, a seed can grow,
A glimmer of hope in the depths below,
And though the shadows may ever reign,
The light within will not wane.

Embrace of the Abyss

In shadowed halls where secrets creep,
And whispers echo dark and deep,
A love was born of cruel design,
Entwined in sin, with hearts malign.

Her eyes, like stars in midnight's veil,
Held promises both sweet and frail,
Yet from her lips, a poison bled,
A kiss of dread, where angels fled.

Beneath the moon's cold, pallid glare,
They danced, a macabre pair,
With every step, the shadows grew,
A specter of the love they knew.

His touch, a shiver down her spine,
A fevered pulse in threads of time,
Yet every caress, a silent scream,
Bound in a never-ending dream.

In crypts of night, their vows were made,
In twilight's grasp, where souls decayed,

A bond unholy, carved in stone,
A love to freeze the marrow bone.

The roses wilted, petals fell,
Each drop of blood a silent knell,
For love that walks in death's embrace,
Finds only sorrow's darkened trace.

The candles flicker, dying light,
Two shadows merge into the night,
In cursed union, lost and damned,
Their love a plague upon the land.

In endless night, their spirits soar,
Forever bound, to love no more,
For in the dark, where shadows kiss,
They found their doom—embrace of the abyss.

In the chambers of my heart, where light resides,
A beacon that flickers, yet never hides,
Born of pain, in shadows it gleams,
A fragile glow amidst silent screams.

Pain carves its path, deep and wide,
A river of sorrow where tears confide,
Yet from these depths, a strength is wrought,
A battle each day, with demons fought.

They whisper lies in the dark of night,
But within me burns a steadfast light,
Against the shadows, I raise my hand,
A warrior's heart, I make my stand.

Each scar a story, each wound a fight,
Against the darkness, for the light,
Pain may bind, but it also frees,
In struggle, I find my heart's keys.

Through the storm, through the rain,
Through the whispers of disdain,
I hold onto the light, fierce and bright,

A guiding star in the blackest night.

For in my heart, where pain has sown,
A garden of light has bravely grown,
Though demons may linger, I remain,
Clinging to the light, to stay sane.

In the silent whispers of my heart's core,
Lies a love untold, boundless and pure,
A tapestry woven with threads of gold,
For a daughter cherished, a tale untold.

This love, a fortress, strong and vast,
A shield eternal, forever to last,
In shadows cast by life's cruel hand,
I stand unwavering, a guardian planned.

From dawn's first light to twilight's end,
My watchful eyes and heart attend,
Through every trial, each stormy tide,
A constant presence by your side.

Unspoken vows in the still of night,
A bond unbreakable, shining bright,
In your laughter, a melody sweet,
In your tears, a pain that I meet.

You are the moon to my endless sky,
The star in the night, my reason why,
Every heartbeat, a silent prayer,
Every breath, a promise to care.

No harm shall breach this sacred space,
No shadow dim your radiant grace,
For in this love, so deeply set,
Lies a strength you won't forget.

As years unfold and time moves fast,
Know this love, a spell ever cast,
A protection vast, through all that's told,
A love unending, forever bold.

Shadows whisper, silent screams,
Twisted dreams in moonlit beams.
Eternal night, stars conceal,
Hushed are hearts that once did feel.

Mist enshrouds the barren trees,
Spirits wander, never free.
Time's cruel hand, cold and stark,
Carves its sorrow in the dark.

Yet even in the deepest night,
Faintest glimmers hint at light.
For in the gloom, the soul can find,
A tranquil peace within the mind.

In the depths of darkness, hope does reside,
A flickering flame, refusing to hide.
With each passing moment, it grows strong,
Defying the shadows, where it belongs.

In the midst of darkness, when skies seem gray,
Remember, beautiful, you'll find your way.
With strength in your heart and courage so strong,
You'll rise above, and prove them wrong.

You're not alone, for I'm here by your side,
Through every tear shed, and every stride.
Believe in yourself, for you're capable and brave,
You'll conquer this storm, and emerge unscathed.

So hold your head high, and keep pushing through,
Know that the sun will shine again for you.
In your heart, find solace, and let it guide,
For brighter days are waiting, just on the other side.

Velvet black, the night unfurled,
A silent world, in darkness swirled.
Nocturnal bloom, with thorns adorned,
Where light is shunned, and day is scorned.

A raven's caw, the only sound,
In this abyss where fears are found.
The ebony tide, relentless, deep,
Swallows secrets that it keeps.

Yet, do not dread the somber hours,
For in the shade, rare beauty flowers.
Embrace the dark, let stars ignite,
Within the void, find your own light.

In twilight's realm, where whispers dwell,
The quietude casts a silent spell.
A canvas vast, of obsidian hue,
Where dreams are lost and born anew.

A spectral dance, the shadows play,
In the waltz of night, 'til break of day.
A world unseen, where echoes lie,
Beneath the watch of a wistful sky.

For in the gloom, where secrets hide,
Is a place where truth and dare collide.
So seek the stars, though veiled they seem,
In the dark, let your spirit dream.

Oh light that dances, bright and free,
A flicker in the dark, a spark to see.
It glides across the shadow's face,
A gentle touch, a warm embrace.

It paints the morning in hues of gold,
A story of the day, yet to be told.
It weaves through leaves, a playful dance,
In every ray, there's a chance.

It whispers secrets to the moon,
A silent song, a quiet tune.
It's the artist of the dawn and dusk,
A brush of glory, in twilight's hush.

In every beam, there's life anew,
A path of hope, a different view.
Oh light, in you we find our way,
A guide, a friend, In night or day.

Due

Draw back, for life lies just ahead,
Like an arrow, keep moving forward,
But like a bullet, we all drop dead,
Life's connection often interrupted.

Disconnected from my emotions,
Like a phone cut off by unpaid bill,
Seeking a fleeting power's motion,
Heartbeat's rhythm, quiet and still.

Temporary pulse until arrest,
No more oxygen within the chest,
Factories of life due for repair,
Can someone save me from this despair?

Determination lies hidden,
Waiting for the cold dawn's embrace,
Hoping to see the new day risen,
Seeking solace in a gentle place.

In the shadowed hallways of his mind,
A soul wanders, fractured, blind.
Echoes of the past entwined,
In guilt's grip, he's confined.

Once a beacon, bright and clear,
Now a phantom held by fear.
Memories sharp as broken glass,
Pierce his heart, they amass.

Regret, a whisper in the dark,
Lit his way, a burning spark.
Every step, a heavy chain,
Bound to sorrow, bound to pain.

The faces lost, the words unsaid,
Dance around his weary head.
Haunted eyes that never sleep,
In the silence, shadows creep.

The weight of wrongs, a crushing blow,
In the depths, he's forced to go.
Searching for a light unseen,
In the realms where guilt is queen.

Oh, if time could mend the scar,
Erase the fault, the wound afar.
But in this labyrinth, he's caught,
By the anguish his mind wrought.

A soul adrift in endless night,
Seeking solace, seeking light.
Yet in the mire, he remains,
A prisoner of his own chains.

Through the storm, through the strife,
In the ruins of his life,
Hope may rise, a fragile dove,
To guide him back to light and love.

In the quiet of the midnight hour,
Lies a heart, both bruised and dour.
Unspoken words, a silent plea,
Love confined, yet yearning free.

Eyes that meet but dare not linger,
Soft caress from timid finger.
In shadows cast by fleeting glance,
A secret love, denied the chance.

The burden of what's left unsaid,
Lays heavy on a heart of lead.
Each moment close, yet far apart,
Leaves a scar upon the heart.

A love that blossoms, never shown,
In silent whispers, seeds are sown.
The ache of longing, held within,
Desire fights a battle grim.

What if the words could find their way,
From heart to lips, in light of day?
Would love then flourish, unrestrained,

Or shatter in the truth's domain?

Yet fear holds tight its bitter grip,
The chance of loss, a trembling lip.
So silence reigns where passion dwells,
In secret thoughts, where no one tells.

In dreams, the love is pure and bright,
But wakes to shadows of the night.
The burden grows with every day,
Unspoken words that waste away.

Oh, to free the heart's desire,
To let the words ignite the fire.
But fear, the keeper of the key,
Locks love away, eternally.

In the silent chambers of my mind,
A shadow lingers, unconfined.
An apology left unsaid,
A burden that I've come to dread.

Moments pass, yet time stands still,
With every heartbeat, a deeper chill.
Regret, a ghost that haunts my days,
In countless, unforgiving ways.

Words I wished to speak aloud,
Remain entombed, a shrouded cloud.
Their absence weaves a tangled thread,
In the tapestry of words unsaid.

The sorrow of a broken bond,
Of bridges burned and love beyond,
Lies heavy on my weary heart,
A wound that never will depart.

Eyes that plead for peace, forgiveness,
Meet with silence, deep and endless.
The chance to mend, to heal, to mend,
Slipped away like grains of sand.

In the echo of what might have been,
Lies the weight of my silent sin.
An apology, so long delayed,
A debt of sorrow yet unpaid.

Now, in the darkness, I reside,
With guilt and grief my constant guide.
For every moment, every breath,
Is marked by this, my living death.

If only time could turn around,
And grace in words once more be found.
But in this life, I'm left to dread,
The silence of what's left unsaid.

In the stillness of the night,
When stars are dim and shadows bite,
I feel the weight of past mistakes,
A burden that my heart forsakes.

Each error made, a heavy stone,
Carved with guilt, and mine alone.
They stack like mountains in my soul,
Consuming all, exacting toll.

Memories that never fade,
Of choices wrong and debts unpaid,
Haunt my dreams and waking hours,
In regret's relentless showers.

What ifs and might have beens,
Echo loud in silent scenes.
Every path I didn't take,
Marks the heart that's apt to break.

Apologies left unsaid,
Bitter words I still dread.
Actions taken in a haze,
Burning through my peaceful days.

Faces lost and trust betrayed,
All the times I walked away.
Promises I couldn't keep,
Tear through nights devoid of sleep.

In the mirror, I see the past,
Reflections that forever last.
A younger me, with hopeful eyes,
Now sees through sorrowed, jaded guise.

Can forgiveness find a way,
To heal the scars, to light the day?
Or am I destined to endure,
The weight of guilt without a cure?

Oh, to turn the hands of time,
To right the wrongs, to stop the climb.
But here I stand, with heavy heart,
Consumed by past that won't depart.

In the twilight's gentle grasp,
Where light and dark together clasp,
Lie shadows of a broken promise,
Echoing through the silent abyss.

Once, in days of golden light,
Words were spoken, hearts took flight.
A vow made strong, a pledge of truth,
Sealed with hope and tender youth.

But time, the thief of dreams and plans,
Unraveled bonds with unseen hands.
Promises once bright and clear,
Faded fast, then disappeared.

Now, in corners dark and still,
Linger shadows cold and chill.
Ghosts of what was meant to be,
Haunt the spaces within me.

Eyes that once shone with belief,
Now reflect a deeper grief.
For trust, once whole, now lies in shards,
Guarded by unyielding guards.

Every whisper of the past,
Brings a pang, a shadow cast.
Memories of love's sweet start,
Now pierce the soul, break the heart.

What could have been, what was not kept,
In quiet moments, deeply wept.
A broken promise, like a scar,
Marks the soul, near and far.

In the silence of the night,
Shadows dance in pale moonlight.
Reminding me of vows once made,
Of love that slipped and slowly strayed.

If only time could mend the breach,
Restore the words, the hearts to reach.
But shadows stay, and promises broken,
Leave behind words unspoken.

Beneath the moon's soft, silvery light,
A heart lies heavy through the night.
Each beat a sigh, each pulse a tear,
Haunted by regrets held near.

Once it danced with joy and grace,
Now it bears a sorrowed face.
Choices made and paths once tread,
Weigh like stones, a constant dread.

Memories, sharp as winter's chill,
Whisper of a long-lost thrill.
Moments missed and words unsaid,
Fill the heart with boundless dread.

Love that faded, dreams that died,
Hopes abandoned, cast aside.
Regret, a shadow, always near,
Filling days with silent fear.

Faces haunt and voices call,
From the depths where sorrows fall.
In the quiet, echoes play,
Of yesterdays that slipped away.

What might have been,
what could have been,
Haunt the spaces deep within.
A heart once light, now burdened sore,
Yearns for peace but finds no more.

If time could heal and wounds could mend,
If broken paths could find their end,
But in the present, all it sees,
Are ghosts of past realities.

So here it beats, with somber tone,
A heart weighed down, forever alone.
With every breath, it mourns the past,
In shadows deep, regrets are cast.

Echoes

In the quiet of the dawn's first light,
When shadows yield to morning's might,
Echoes of lost love still play,
Haunting whispers of a yesterday.

Once, where hearts entwined with grace,
Lies an empty, hollowed space.
Memories of laughter's song,
Now a silence, deep and long.

Eyes that once held tender fire,
Now reflect a cold, quenching mire.
Touches soft as morning dew,
Vanished in a grayish hue.

Every corner of this place,
Bears the ghost of your embrace.
Whispers soft, a lover's plea,
Fade into eternity.

Footsteps echo down the hall,
In the spaces where we'd fall.

Hands once clasped, now drift apart,
Tearing gently at the heart.

Moonlit nights and starry skies,
Hold the tears of long goodbyes.
Promises that slipped away,
Echo in the light of day.

If only time could heal the break,
Reverse the steps of each mistake.
But in this life, we're left to mourn,
Love that's lost and dreams that's torn.

In the silence, hear the call,
Of love that's lost, of hearts that fall.
Echoes drift on winds above,
A symphony of lost love.

Remorse

In the quiet depths of night,
Where shadows merge with pale moonlight,
Lies a heart, in sorrow bound,
Remorse within, without a sound.

Silence thick, a heavy veil,
Where whispered winds and secrets sail.
Each breath a sigh, each thought a tear,
Regret's embrace, so close, so near.

Eyes that stare into the dark,
Search for peace, a fleeting spark.
Memories sharp as winter's bite,
Pierce the calm of endless night.

Words unsaid and deeds undone,
Haunt the hours 'til the dawn.
Every heartbeat, every thought,
Wrestles with the pain it's wrought.

Faces from the past arise,
In the stillness of closed eyes.

Ghosts of moments lost in time,
Echo soft, a mournful chime.

If only time could be reversed,
To right the wrongs, to quench the thirst.
But in the night, regret must stay,
A shadow that won't fade away.

Loneliness, a silent friend,
Keeps vigil 'til the night shall end.
With every star, a tear is shed,
For choices made, for words unsaid.

In this quiet, deep and vast,
Lies the sorrow of the past.
Remorse, a never-ending fight,
In the solemn quiet of the night.

Guilty mind

In the chambers of a guilty mind,
Where shadows dance, and whispers bind,
Lies a soul burdened, heavy, and worn,
By the weight of deeds, forever mourned.

Ghosts of choices, mistakes made,
Haunt the corridors where memories fade.
Each step taken, a hesitant tread,
In the labyrinth of thoughts, fear is fed.

Eyes that close, yet never find rest,
Haunted by visions, a relentless quest.
Echoes of words, sharp and unkind,
Wound the heart, torment the mind.

In the stillness of the darkest hour,
Regret takes hold, its grip devour.
Every heartbeat, a drumming refrain,
A symphony of guilt, a melody of pain.

If only time could grant reprieve,
And grant the solace we so believe.

But in this realm where shadows reign,
Remorse and guilt forever remain.

A prisoner of the mind's cruel grasp,
Caught in a cycle, an endless rasp.
Haunted by the choices left behind,
In the haunting of a guilty mind.

Unforgiven

In the quiet of the twilight's sigh,
Where stars ignite the darkened sky,
Fall tears for the unforgiven, lost,
Their stories etched in shadows crossed.

Each tear a whisper, soft and true,
For souls who never found their due.
In silent rivers, they cascade,
For those whose debts were never paid.

Eyes that weep for sins untold,
For secrets kept, for hearts grown cold.
Each drop a prayer, a silent plea,
For mercy's touch to set them free.

In the depths where regrets reside,
Tears fall for those who never tried,
To seek redemption, to make amends,
To find forgiveness, to make new friends.

But in the silence, they remain,
Bound by shackles, wracked with pain.

Their tears a river, deep and wide,
For the unforgiven, who never died.

In the twilight's gentle embrace,
Their tears fall softly, leaving no trace.
But in the echoes of the night,
Their sorrow lingers, a fading light.

So let us weep for those unseen,
For the unforgiven, caught between,
The past and future, night and day,
Tears for them, we gently pray.

Sorrow

In the shadows of a somber tale,
Lies a life where sorrows prevail.
Each day a burden, heavy to bear,
Consumed by grief, consumed by despair.

From dawn to dusk, the tears do flow,
In the heart of darkness, where whispers go.
A life defined by the weight of sorrow,
Where joy is fleeting, and hope, tomorrow.

Memories, like ghosts, haunt the mind,
Of loves lost and dreams left behind.
Regrets, like chains, bind the soul,
In the depths where sadness takes its toll.

Faces etched with lines of pain,
Eyes that weep like summer rain.
Each breath a sigh, each heartbeat a sigh,
In the landscape of sadness, where dreams do die.

Oh, to find solace, to find release,

From the grip of grief, from the ache that won't cease.
But in the silence, the sorrow remains,
A constant companion, through life's trials and pains.

Yet in the depths, a flicker of light,
A glimmer of hope, shining bright.
For even in sorrow, there's strength to be found,
In the hearts that rise, when darkness surrounds.

So let us hold onto the threads of grace,
And let love's light illuminate the space.
 For though life may be defined by sorrow and grief,
In the end, it's love that brings relief.

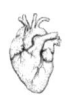

Grip of guilt

In the depths of the soul, where shadows lie,
Resides a specter, with a mournful cry.
The relentless grip of guilt, its hold so tight,
A shadowy figure in the dead of night.

It whispers in the silence, a haunting tune,
A constant reminder of deeds undone.
Each step taken, each breath drawn,
The weight of guilt, a burden borne.

Memories like daggers, sharp and cold,
Pierce the heart, leaving stories untold.
The echoes of mistakes, they never fade,
In the relentless grip of guilt, they're arrayed.

Eyes that search for solace, find only pain,
In the endless cycle of remorse's reign.
A prisoner of the past, with no reprieve,
In the relentless grip of guilt, we grieve.

Oh, to break free from its suffocating hold,
To find redemption in a future untold.

But the grip of guilt, it knows no end,
A relentless foe, on which we depend.

Yet in the depths of despair, a flicker of light,
A glimmer of hope, shining bright.
For forgiveness waits, a beacon in the night,
To guide us from the relentless grip of guilt's blight.

Memories

In the corners of the mind, they reside,
Memories that refuse to subside.
Like timeless treasures, they gleam and shine,
Echoes of moments, frozen in time.

Each one a thread in life's tapestry,
A mosaic of moments, vast and free.
From the laughter of youth to the tears of old,
Memories weave stories, precious and bold.

The scent of a rose in a summer breeze,
The touch of a loved one, gentle and ease.
The taste of a childhood treat, sweet and pure,
Memories linger, steadfast and sure.

In the silence of night, they softly call,
Whispers of love, echoing through all.
They dance in dreams and linger in day,
Memories that never fade away.

Through trials and triumphs, they remain,
An eternal beacon, a guiding flame.

For in the tapestry of life, they're made,
Memories that never fade, but gently cascade.

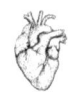

Misdeed

In the ledger of life, a debt is sown,
For every misdeed, a price is known.
A coin of regret, heavy and steep,
Paid in the currency of sorrow, deep.

With every choice, a ripple cast,
The consequences, they hold steadfast.
For actions taken, in haste or heed,
Demand a price, a reckoning deed.

The cost may be hidden, yet it remains,
A shadow that lingers, a mark that stains.
In the hearts of those who've been betrayed,
The price of a misdeed is never repaid.

It echoes in the silence, a haunting call,
A reminder of the downfall.
For what is lost can't be regained,
The price of a misdeed, forever retained.

Yet in the darkness, a glimmer of light,
A chance for redemption, to make things right.

To own up to the wrongs, to mend the breach,
And pay the price, to find release.

For though the cost may be steep indeed,
There's solace in the act of heed.
To learn and grow from mistakes made,
Is the true price of a misdeed, well paid.

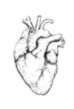

Maze

In the maze of remorse, where shadows creep,
Lost souls wander, their secrets to keep.
Each twist and turn, a path of regret,
In the labyrinth of sorrow, where memories set.

Whispers of could haves and should haves resound,
In the corridors of guilt, where sorrows abound.
Faces of loved ones, etched with pain,
In the maze of remorse, they leave their stain.

Each wrong turn leads to deeper despair,
In the labyrinth of remorse, with no solace to spare.
Echoes of past mistakes, they echo and wail,
In the corridors of regret, where darkness prevails.

But amidst the chaos, a flicker of light,
A glimmer of hope in the darkest of night.
For in the maze of remorse, there's a way out,
If one can find courage to dispel doubt.

With each step forward, the shadows recede,

In the labyrinth of remorse, there's room to concede.
To forgive oneself, to let go of the past,
Is the key to escape, to find peace at last.

So in the maze of remorse, let us not despair,
For there's always a way out, if we dare.
To embrace forgiveness, to walk in grace,
Is to find redemption, in this sacred space.

Lost chances

In the hush of twilight's tender glow,
Where dreams take flight, and sorrows flow,
Lies the sorrow of lost chances, unclaimed,
A haunting melody, forever unnamed.

Each missed opportunity, a whispered sigh,
In the quiet moments, where regrets lie.
The road not taken, the words unsaid,
In the sorrow of lost chances, hearts are led.

Eyes that gaze upon the fading light,
Recall the moments, slipped from sight.
Hands that reach for what's no longer there,
Feel the weight of lost chances, heavy and rare.

In the tapestry of life, they weave their thread,
The sorrow of lost chances, where dreams tread.
For what could have been, and what might be,
Lingers in the heart, for all to see.

But in the sorrow, there's a bittersweet grace,
A reminder of life's ever- changing pace.

For in the loss, there's room to grow,
To seize the chances that tomorrow may bestow.

So let us not dwell on what's been missed,
But embrace the journey, with each twist.
For in the sorrow of lost chances, we find,
The strength to move forward, with heart and mind.

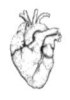

Redemption

In the depths of despair, where shadows loom,
A soul seeks redemption, amid the gloom.
Lost in the labyrinth of its own making,
Yearning for solace, for light in the breaking.

With each weary step, it seeks a way out,
From the chains of guilt, from the shackles of doubt.
In the quiet of night, it whispers a prayer,
Hoping for mercy, for someone to care.

For every misdeed, every wrong turn,
The soul bears the burden, the lessons to learn.
But in the darkness, there's a flicker of hope,
A glimmer of light on the treacherous slope.

With courage renewed, it faces the past,
Confronting the demons that held it fast.
Seeking forgiveness, both from within and without,
The soul journeys on, amidst the doubt.

For redemption is not an easy road,

Filled with trials and burdens untold.
But with each step forward, it finds release,
And in the journey, it discovers peace.

So let us walk with the soul seeking light,
Guiding it through the darkest night.
For in the quest for redemption, we find,
A path to healing, for heart and mind.

Torment

Within the depths where shadows reign,
Resides the torment, the inner pain.
Demons lurk with twisted grin,
Feeding on the chaos within.

Whispers in the silence of the night,
Echoes of fears, the endless fight.
They claw and tear, relentless, keen,
Filling the mind with visions unseen.

Each doubt, each worry, they amplify,
In the caverns of the soul, they lie.
Haunting dreams and restless sleep,
Inner demons, their vigil keep.

They whisper lies of worthlessness,
Of failures past, of hopelessness.
Their grip so tight, their hold so strong,
They dance and revel, all night long.

But in the heart, a flicker of light,
A glimmer of hope in the endless night.

For courage rises, against the tide,
To face the demons, to cast aside.

With strength and will, the battle's fought,
Against the demons, both feared and sought.
For in the depths, where shadows loom,
Lies the strength to banish gloom.

So face the torment, the inner strife,
And find the courage to claim your life.
For though the demons may torment and tease,
You hold the power to set your soul at ease.

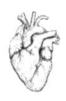

In the stillness of the night's embrace,
Where shadows linger, leaving no trace,
Lies the silence of regret, profound and deep,
In the heart's chamber, where memories keep.

A whispered sigh, a mournful tone,
Echoes of choices, now overgrown.
In the quiet, where words remain unsaid,
Regret's heavy silence, hangs like lead.

Each moment passed, each opportunity lost,
Leaves a mark, like frost on a cost.
The weight of what could have been,
Bears down on the soul, relentless, keen.

In the silence, the mind replays,
The scenes of yesteryears, in endless arrays.
The words left unspoken, the deeds left undone,
Haunt the heart, until the morning sun.

Oh, the silence of regret, it speaks volumes,
In the echo of choices, like silent tombs.
Yet amidst the silence, there's a glimmer of light,

A chance to mend, to make things right.

For in the silence of regret, there lies,
The seed of wisdom, the chance to rise.
To learn from the past, to embrace the pain,
And in the silence, find peace again.

Beneath the veil of trust's sweet guise,
Lies the cost of betrayal, a bitter prize.
A wound so deep, it cuts to the core,
Leaving scars that ache forevermore.

In the garden of friendship, where flowers bloom,
Lurks the specter of betrayal, a shadowed gloom.
Each whispered secret, each shared vow,
Shattered in the moment of betrayal's now.

The cost is high, the toll severe,
When trust is broken, and bonds disappear.
For what once was solid, now crumbles to dust,
Leaving hearts in turmoil, lost and thrust.

The pain of betrayal, it knows no end,
A wound that festers, a foe to contend.
In the echoes of lies, in the shadows cast,
The cost of betrayal, it lingers fast.

Yet amidst the wreckage, there's a glimmer of light,
A chance to heal, to make things right.
For forgiveness, though hard to find,

Can mend the wounds, and soothe the mind.

So let us beware, of the cost so steep,
And cherish the trust that we choose to keep.
For in the end, it's the bonds we hold dear,
That are worth more than any cost of betrayal's fear.

Under twilight's tender embrace,
The unforgiving conscience takes its place.
Whispers in the quiet, haunting the night,
A relentless knell, devoid of light.

Each misstep, a weight upon the soul,
No respite found, no mercy to console.
In the corridors of guilt, it dwells,
A constant reminder of deeds that compel.

A burden heavy, upon the chest it lies,
No escape from the guilt, no compromise.
Every heartbeat echoes with remorse,
In the unforgiving conscience's course.

Yet amidst the darkness, a glimmer of light,
A chance for redemption, to make things right.
For even the unforgiving conscience may yield,
To the power of forgiveness, in love revealed.

So let us face the shadows with courage and grace,
For in the depths of the soul, there's room to embrace.
With each step forward, may we find release,

From the grip of the unforgiving conscience, at peace.

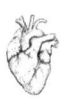

Lie the corridors of memory's domain,
Lingers the ghost of past errors, a haunting refrain.
Whispers of mistakes, echoes of regret,
In the chambers of the mind, they linger yet.

Each misstep, a specter in the shadows' dance,
A haunting reminder of a fateful chance.
The ghost of past errors, it looms so near,
Filling the heart with sorrow, with fear.

In the quiet of night, it whispers its tale,
Of choices made and hopes that failed.
The ghost of past errors, it knows no rest,
A constant presence, a relentless test.

Every heartbeat, a reminder of the past,
Of roads not taken, of dreams that didn't last.
The ghost of past errors, it weighs heavy still,
A burden on the soul, a bitter pill.

Yet amidst the darkness, there shines a light,
A beacon of hope, in the darkest night.
For in the ghost of past errors, there lies,

The seeds of wisdom, the chance to rise.

To learn from mistakes, to embrace the pain,
And in the ghost of past errors, find gain.
For though it may haunt, it also can teach,
To reach for redemption, within our reach.

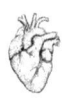

Beneath the shattered sky of dusk's demise,
Lies the wreckage of trust, in silent cries.
Broken fragments strewn upon the ground,
A shattered bond, nowhere to be found.

Once, it stood tall, a fortress strong,
Guarding hearts from all that's wrong.
But cracks appeared, and trust gave way,
To the weight of doubts, that led astray.

In the echoes of promises, now shattered,
Lies the pain of trust, forever tattered.
Each shard a memory, sharp and cold,
Of vows broken, of stories untold.

Eyes that once sparkled, now dim with tears,
As shattered trust fills the heart with fears.
Hands that reached out, now pull away,
From the shards of trust, in disarray.

In the silence of betrayal's aftermath,
Lies the sorrow of trust's broken path.
For what was once whole, now lies in ruins,

A shattered trust, beneath the moon's glow's loom.

Yet amidst the rubble, there lies a chance,
To rebuild trust, to heal and enhance.
For from broken pieces, new bonds may rise,
Stronger and wiser, under clearer skies.

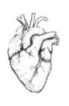

In the silence of the heart's hollow,
Echoes the pain of a broken vow.
Once, it stood as a beacon bright,
Guiding souls through darkest night.

Promises made, in vows untold,
Now shattered, like glass, cold and old.
Each word spoken, with love and care,
Now lies broken, beyond repair.

The pain of a broken vow, once whole,
Lingers on, taking its toll.
Like a wound that never seems to heal,
It festers deep, refusing to reveal.

Eyes that once gleamed with hope's light,
Now clouded with tears, dimmed by night.
Hands that once clasped with tender grace,
Now ache with the memory, a bitter embrace.

In the quiet of the soul's despair,
The pain of a broken vow, so unfair.
For what was once whole, now lies in pieces,

Scattered by the winds of doubt and deceases.

Yet amidst the pain, there's a glimmer of hope,
A chance to mend what fate has broke.
For from the ashes of broken vows,
New beginnings may arise, somehow.

Behind the bars of a somber mind,
Lies the prison of regret, cruel and unkind.
Walls built high with whispers of past,
Each memory a stone, meant to last.

Locked within, a heart heavy with pain,
Haunted by choices that can't be reclaimed.
Echoes of moments, decisions once made,
Resound through the halls where shadows invade.

Glimmers of sunlight struggle to break,
Through the darkness of each mistake.
Chains of "what ifs" and "should have beens,"
Bind the soul in an endless spin.

No key to unlock, no window to see,
A world without guilt, a mind set free.
In the prison of regret, time stands still,
Filling the silence with an aching chill.

Yet deep within, beneath the despair,
Lies a spark of hope, flickering there.
For every prison has a door to find,

And redemption awaits in a forgiving mind.

So though the bars may seem to hold tight,
Within the heart burns a guiding light.
To forgive oneself, to let go of the pain,
And break free from the prison of regret's reign.

Underneath a calm facade's veil,
Lies the sting of a harsh word's trail.
Sharp and sudden, like a thorn,
Leaving the heart tattered and torn.

In the moment it is spoken,
A bond of trust can be broken.
The echo of the cutting sound,
Lingers long, profoundly profound.

Eyes that once sparkled with delight,
Now dim with the weight of the slight.
A smile that once graced gentle lips,
Now falters, as confidence slips.

The harsh word, like a poison dart,
Strikes deep within, wounds the heart.
Its venom spreads, slow and wide,
Turning joy to sorrow inside.

Yet amid the pain, there's room to heal,
To find the strength, the wounds to seal.
For words of kindness, tender and true,

Can mend the soul, renew what's due.

Let us be mindful of words we choose,
Aware of the power they can use.
For though a harsh word can bring such sting,
A word of love can make hearts sing.

Amidst the twisting paths, so tight,
Lost in the labyrinth of guilt's dark night.
Walls that loom and shadows that blend,
A maze with no clear start or end.

Each step taken, a burden increased,
Memories of past wrongs never released.
Echoes of errors, whispers of blame,
Haunt the corridors, calling my name.

Seeking escape, yet finding no way,
Lost in the labyrinth, I wander and stray.
The weight of guilt, a relentless chain,
Binding my spirit, inflicting pain.

Corners turned and paths retraced,
Haunted by choices, and time misplaced.
Regret like a fog, thick and cold,
In this labyrinth, my heart is sold.

No light to guide, no compass to steer,
Only the shadows of guilt draw near.
Yet in the distance, a glimmer so slight,

A beacon of hope, piercing the night.

To find forgiveness, to let go of shame,
To leave behind the constant blame.
For within the labyrinth, there's a chance to heal,
To confront the guilt, to make it real.

Lost in the labyrinth, but not without fight,
I strive towards that distant light.
For in the journey, the soul can find,
The path to peace, and a clearer mind.

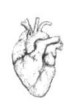

In the remnants of a life, once whole,
Lie the ruins of a fractured soul.
Scattered pieces of dreams once bright,
Now lost in the shadows of endless night.

Broken promises and shattered dreams,
Echoes of pain in silent screams.
Each crack a wound, each fracture a scar,
Testaments to battles fought afar.

In the ruins, a heart lies torn,
By the weight of the burdens born.
Memories linger, haunting the air,
A ghostly presence, a solemn prayer.

Yet amidst the rubble, a glimmer of light,
A beacon of hope in the darkest night.
For from the ruins, strength may arise,
 A phoenix reborn, soaring the skies.

Gather the pieces, one by one,
For in the brokenness, new life begun.
Embrace the scars, let them tell,

The story of a soul that has risen from hell.

In the ruins of a fractured life,
Lies the potential to overcome strife.
To rebuild, to heal, to find grace,
And stand once more in the light's embrace.

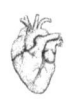

Lie within tapestry of time, a thread undone,
A missed opportunity, a race not won.
The sorrow it brings, like a heavy weight,
Dragging the spirit, sealing fate.

In the quiet moments, it whispers its tale,
Of what could have been, of dreams set to sail.
The road not taken, the chance not seized,
Leaves the heart heavy, the soul appeased.

Eyes that search for what's now out of reach,
Grasping at shadows, longing to breach.
Hands that yearn to grasp the elusive prize,
Find only emptiness, beneath the skies.

Yet in the sorrow, there's a lesson to learn,
To cherish each moment, to let it burn.
For in the missed opportunity's wake,
New paths may open, new chances take.

So let not the sorrow of missed opportunity weigh,
But rather, let it guide, and light the way.
For in the depths of regret, there lies,

The seed of resilience, ready to rise.

Weighty burdens borne in silence's thrall,
The quiet apology, held like a pall.
Unspoken words, heavy with remorse,
A burden carried, a hidden force.

In the depths of the soul, it quietly resides,
The weight of the apology, where guilt abides.
Each unsaid word, a heavy load,
On shoulders bent, on hearts corrode.

The silence speaks volumes, louder than words,
Aching with sorrow, like silent birds.
Eyes downcast, avoiding the gaze,
Carrying the weight of unspoken phrase.

Yet in the silence, there's a stirring plea,
For forgiveness to set the burden free.
To break the silence, to speak the truth,
And release the weight, where shadows dance,
A nocturnal symphony, a moonlit trance.

Each moonbeam a spotlight, on the stage,
In the moon's embrace, we engage.
Silver light bathes the earth below,

Casting a mystical, ethereal glow.

Whispers of the night, soft and clear,
Echoing secrets we hold dear.
Owls hoot in distant trees,
Their calls harmonize with the evening breeze.

Crickets serenade with a rhythmic tune,
Nature's orchestra under the moon.
The cool night air is a gentle kiss,
A moment of calm, a pure, quiet bliss.

Stars twinkle in the velvet sky,
Guardians of dreams, as night goes by.
Fireflies flicker in playful flight,
Adding sparkle to the tranquil night.

Their tiny lanterns, a magical sight,
Guiding hearts with their soft, warm light.
Footsteps on a moonlit path,
Softly tread with gentle wrath.

Each step a promise, a journey begun,
Beneath the moonlight, we are one.
As night deepens, the world finds rest,
Nature cradled in the moon's soft nest.

Dreams take flight, in the cool, calm air,
Beneath the moonlight, free from care.
The night hums with a serene, quiet might,
A timeless moment, pure and bright.

In this lunar glow, we find our grace,
Beneath the moonlight, in its embrace.

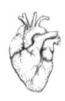

I lay in the stillness of my soul, echoes resound,
Whispers of regret, sorrow unbound.
Each beat of my heart, a mournful cry,
Echoes of mistakes, reaching for the sky.

I carry the weight of choices made,
In the echoes of regret, I'm afraid.
Each echo a reminder of paths not taken,
Of dreams abandoned, of hearts forsaken.

In the darkness of my mind, echoes play,
A haunting melody, day by day.
In the silence of night, beneath the moon,
I'm haunted by echoes of my own tune.

Eyes once bright, now clouded with tears,
For moments lost, for wasted years.
My regretful heart, it dwells in shadow,
Caught in the echoes of my own sorrow.

Yet amidst the echoes, there's a glimmer,
A chance to rise, a chance to shimmer.
To learn from my mistakes, to start anew,

And bid farewell to the echoes of rue.

Let the echoes fade into the night,
As I find the courage to seek the light.
For in the echoes of my regretful heart's sigh,
Lies the strength to forgive, and let go, and fly.

Under the soul's vast expanse, a quest ignites,
Unfolding in the shadows, seeking guiding lights.
A soul, adrift in chaos, craves serene release,
A yearning for tranquility, a longing for peace.

Through valleys deep and canyons wide, it wanders,
Amidst the tempest's roar, its purpose ponders.
Seeking solace 'neath the stars, in twilight's embrace,
Longing for serenity, amidst life's bustling race.

In the silence of the night, it finds a whispering guide,
A melody of hope, where shadows hide.
A beacon of peace, a distant, guiding star,
Leading the soul from darkness, toward a realm afar.

Through trials and tribulations, it forges its way,
Confronting doubts and fears, come what may.
For peace isn't merely absence, but a spirit's choice,
To embrace life's tumult, and find its voice.

With each step forward, closer to its quest,
The soul persists, through trials and tests.
In the gentle cradle of its own embrace,
It discovers solace, and a tranquil grace.

So let the journey unfurl, let the soul roam free,
In its pursuit of peace, may it forever be.
For as it charts its course, through night and day,
May peace be its companion, come what may.

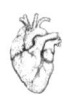

Through the darkest of times, it softly sings,
A melody of courage, spreading its wings.
In the depths of despair, where all seems lost,
It offers a lifeline, no matter the cost.

In the quiet moments, when tears are shed,
It whispers of strength, lifting the head.
When the world seems bleak, and skies are gray,
It paints a rainbow, lighting the way.

In the heart of the weary, it finds a home,
A flicker of light, where seeds are sown.
For in the whispers of hope, there lies the key,
To unlock the doors, and set the spirit free.

So let it be heard, this whisper so clear,
Banishing doubts, dispelling fear.
For in its gentle cadence, there's power untold,
In the whispers of hope, hearts find gold.

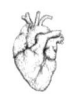

Stars in the Night Sky

In the vast expanse of the night, where stars gleam,
A tapestry of dreams, a celestial scheme.
Each star a story, written in light,
Guiding wanderers through the darkest night.

Twinkling diamonds scattered across the velvet sky,
Each one a beacon, a promise to defy.
Their shimmering beauty ignites the imagination,
A cosmic ballet, a celestial sensation.

Constellations weave tales of ancient lore,
Their shapes etched in the heavens forevermore.
From Orion's belt to the Big Dipper's arc,
Each constellation leaves its celestial mark.

The Milky Way stretches like a cosmic river,
A highway of stars where dreams deliver.
Its ethereal glow illuminates the night,
A reminder of the universe's endless might.

As night descends and darkness falls,
The stars above answer nature's calls.

They twinkle and shimmer, in endless array,
Guiding souls through the night until the break of day.

For in the vast expanse of the night, where stars gleam,
A tapestry of dreams, a celestial scheme.
Each star a story, written in light,
Guiding wanderers through the darkest night.

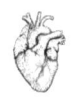

Flames of Passion

In the heart's embrace, where passions ignite,
A dance of flames, burning bright.
Each flicker a yearning, a desire untamed,
Fueling the soul, unashamed.

The flames leap and dance, in a fiery trance,
A mesmerizing display of passion's advance.
Their warmth envelops, like a lover's touch,
Igniting the senses, craving it much.

In the depths of the soul, where desires reside,
The flames of passion cannot be denied.
They flicker and flare, with each beat of the heart,
A fiery dance, an intimate art.

The crackle of flames, a hypnotic sound,
Echoes the intensity, all around.
As embers glow and sparks take flight,
The passion within burns through the night.

In the flickering glow, shadows play,
As lovers entwine in passion's sway.

Their hearts ablaze with fiery delight,
Lost in the flames, burning bright.

For in the heart's embrace, where passions ignite,
A dance of flames, burning bright.
Each flicker a testament, to love's flame,
Burning eternal, in passion's name.

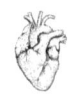

Echoes of the Canyon

In the canyon's depths, where echoes roam,
A chorus of voices, finding home.
Each echo a memory, a tale to tell,
Carved in stone, where echoes dwell.

The canyon walls rise, majestic and tall,
Echoing the whispers, the cries, the call.
Each crevice and cavern, a keeper of lore,
Echoes of the past, forevermore.

As footsteps echo through the narrow pass,
The canyon whispers secrets, like shards of glass.
Each rock and stone, a witness to time,
Echoing stories, both yours and mine.

In the silence of the canyon, where echoes rebound,
Voices of the past, can still be found.
The laughter, the tears, the joy, the pain,
Echoing through the canyon's domain.

As sunlight filters through the rocky clefts,
Casting shadows like silhouetted thefts,

The echoes bounce from wall to wall,
A symphony of memory, answering the call.

In the canyon's depths, where echoes reside,
The past and present intertwine, side by side.
Each echo a reminder, of where we've been,
Carving the canyon of our lives within.

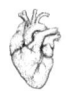

Dawn's Embrace

As the sun rises, painting the sky,
A new day dawns, where dreams can fly.
With each golden ray, hope is born,
In dawn's embrace, a new morn.

Birdsong fills the crisp morning air,
A melody of life, tender and fair.
The world awakens from night's deep sleep,
Promises of the day, for hearts to keep.

Dewdrops sparkle on blades of grass,
Glimmering jewels as the moments pass.
Each one a reflection of morning's light,
A symbol of renewal, pure and bright.

Shadows retreat as light takes hold,
A canvas of colors, red and gold.
With every moment, potential unfolds,
Stories of life, yet to be told.

Mountains bask in the sun's first kiss,
Valleys echo with nature's bliss.

Rivers gleam in the soft, warm glow,
Flowing with dreams, where hopes can grow.

People stir from their slumbered state,
Greeting the dawn, embracing fate.
With hearts full of dreams, they start anew,
In the morning's light, all things are true.

As the sun climbs higher in the sky,
The promise of dawn does not lie.
In its embrace, we find our way,
A chance to begin, a brand-new day.

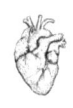

Whispers of the Wind

In the whispers of the wind, secrets hide,
Carried on breezes, far and wide.
Each gust a tale, whispered with care,
In the wind's embrace, stories share.

Among the swaying trees, leaves rustle soft,
A chorus of murmurs, carried aloft.
The wind tells tales of lands afar,
Of deserts, forests, and mountains that scar.

Across the fields, it sweeps with grace,
A touch so gentle, a fleeting embrace.
Grasses bend and bow in silent dance,
Swaying to the wind's mysterious romance.

Through open windows, it whispers low,
Secrets of places we may never know.
It brings the scent of the ocean's spray,
And hints of adventures far away.

On lonely nights, it sings a tune,
A haunting melody beneath the moon.

Its voice, a comfort, a soothing balm,
Easing the heart, bringing calm.

In bustling cities, it finds its way,
Between the buildings, in playful sway.
It gathers the voices, the sounds of life,
Weaving them into a tapestry, free of strife.

On mountaintops, it howls with might,
A powerful force, a sheer delight.
It speaks of strength and timeless grace,
Of nature's wonders, of time's own pace.

Through the desert, it moves like a ghost,
Silent yet present, a constant host.
Shaping the dunes, crafting the sand,
Leaving its mark on the barren land.

In the whispers of the wind, dreams take flight,
Carried across the world, through day and night.
It speaks to the heart, in a language so old,
Tales of the world, in whispers told.

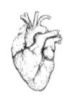

Footsteps in the Sand

Along the shore, where waves caress,
Footsteps in the sand, a timeless dress.
Each print a memory, left behind,
In the sands of time, forever entwined.

The ocean's song, a gentle hum,
Accompanies each step, where we come from.
Footprints fade as the tide sweeps in,
Erasing the past, where we've been.

Yet some remain, as markers true,
Of journeys taken, of skies once blue.
Soft sand beneath, a tender touch,
Each step a story, saying so much.

Seashells glisten, scattered around,
Treasures of the sea, where dreams are found.
Footsteps lead to endless views,
The horizon whispers, of paths to choose.

Morning light casts a golden hue,
On footsteps fresh, as if brand new.

As the day unfolds, the sand will tell,
Of moments lived, and those who dwell.

Each footprint a whisper, of lives we trace,
In the sand's embrace, a fleeting grace.
For in the steps we take, both small and grand,
Lives the story of our journey, etched in the sand.

Silent Symphony

In the quiet of the night, where stars align,
A silent symphony, divine.
Each twinkling star, a note so clear,
In the cosmic orchestra, we hear.

Moonlight bathes the earth in silver hue,
Casting shadows, a dreamy view.
The night air still, a tranquil sea,
In silence, whispers of eternity.

Crickets add their gentle song,
To the silent symphony, where they belong.
Owls hoot softly, a distant call,
Nature's musicians, one and all.

Rustling leaves join the serenade,
A symphony of night, carefully made.
Each breeze a whisper, each sound a thread,
Weaving a tapestry where dreams are fed.

The constellations, bright and bold,
Stories of old in their patterns unfold.

Orion's belt and the Pleiades' light,
Guide us through the silent night.

A shooting star streaks across the sky,
A fleeting note, as it passes by.
In this quiet concert, hearts find peace,
From the symphony of stars, worries cease.

Lying beneath this celestial show,
Thoughts drift softly, like the glow.
In the harmony of night, souls find rest,
In this silent symphony, we are blessed.

In the quiet of the night, where stars align,
A silent symphony, so divine.
Each twinkling star, a note so clear,
In the cosmic orchestra, we draw near.

Whispers of Autumn

As leaves fall gently, from the trees,
Whispers of autumn, carried on the breeze.
Each rustle a reminder, of seasons past,
In autumn's embrace, memories last.

Golden hues and crimson light,
Paint the world in colors bright.
The crisp air whispers tales untold,
Of summers gone, and days of old.

Pumpkins glow in fields of gold,
Harvests gathered, warmth in the cold.
In every falling leaf, we see,
The cycle of life, in harmony.

Bonfires crackle, their embers bright,
Warming hearts on chilly nights.
In the whispers of the autumn wind,
We find the peace that lies within.

As days grow short and nights extend,
Autumn's whispers softly blend,

With memories cherished, futures planned,
In autumn's gentle, loving hand.

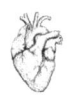

Ripples on the Pond

In the stillness of the pond, where waters lie,
Ripples on the surface catch the eye.
Each ripple a whisper, a story untold,
In the pond's reflection, secrets unfold.

A pebble dropped creates a dance,
Circles widening, given a chance.
The water moves with gentle grace,
Mirroring life's delicate pace.

Dragonflies skim above the sheen,
Glistening wings in the sunlight's beam.
Lily pads float, a tranquil scene,
In   this   quiet pond, serene.

Reflections of trees and sky so blue,
Blend with the ripples, a shifting view.
The pond holds the sky's embrace,
Capturing moments, leaving no trace.

As the breeze stirs, a gentle sigh,
Ripples carry whispers, by and by.

Each wave a connection, past to present,
In the pond's calm, every moment's crescent.

Evening falls with a soft, warm glow,
Ripples fade as the winds slow.
In the stillness of the pond, peace is found,
In nature's gentle, silent sound.

Beneath the Moonlight

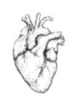

Beneath the moonlight, where shadows dance,
A nocturnal symphony, a moonlit trance.
Each moonbeam a spotlight, on the stage,
In the moon's embrace, we engage.

Silver light bathes the earth below,
Casting a mystical, ethereal glow.
Whispers of the night, soft and clear,
Echoing secrets we hold dear.

Owls hoot in distant trees,
Their calls harmonize with the evening breeze.
Crickets serenade with a rhythmic tune,
Nature's orchestra under the moon.

The cool night air is a gentle kiss,
A moment of calm, a pure, quiet bliss.
Stars twinkle in the velvet sky,
Guardians of dreams, as night goes by.

Fireflies flicker in playful flight,
Adding sparkle to the tranquil night.

Their tiny lanterns, a magical sight,
Guiding hearts with their soft, warm light.

Footsteps on a moonlit path,
Softly tread with gentle wrath.
Each step a promise, a journey begun,
Beneath the moonlight, we are one.

As night deepens, the world finds rest,
Nature cradled in the moon's soft nest.
Dreams take flight,in the cool, calm air,
Beneath the moonlight, free from care.

The night hums with a serene, quiet might,
A timeless moment, pure and bright.
In this lunar glow, we find our grace,
Beneath the moonlight, in its embrace.

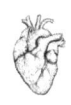

Whispers of Winter

In the hush of winter, where snowflakes fall,
Whispers of winter, a frosty call.
Each snowflake a whisper, in the cold,
In winter's grip, stories unfold.

Trees stand bare, their branches white,
Outlined against the starry night.
Icicles glisten, like crystal wands,
Nature's art, sculpted by frigid hands.

Snow blankets the earth in a peaceful shroud,
A silent world, both still and proud.
Footsteps crunch on the frozen ground,
Echoing softly, a solitary sound.

Chimneys puff with gentle smoke,
Homes aglow, hearts they stoke.
Inside, fires crackle with warmth and cheer,
Shielding us from winter's spear.

Frost etches patterns on windowpanes,
Delicate designs, where beauty reigns.

The wind whispers tales of ancient lore,
Carried across the frozen moor.

Children's laughter fills the air,
Building snowmen with care.
Sleds glide down hills with joyous cries,
Underneath the winter skies.

The nights are long, yet stars 1shine bright,
Guiding souls through the cold, dark night.
The moon casts a serene, silver glow,
Reflecting off the pristine snow.

In winter's whisper, we find repose,
A time for reflection, as nature slows.
Though the cold may bite, and the winds may howl,
In winter's grip, we find a gentle soul.

Fireside warmth, with stories shared,
A time to cherish those who cared.
In the hush of winter, bonds grow tight,
Whispers of love in the cold, dark night.

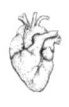

Waves of Serenity

By the ocean's edge, where the waves meet the shore,
A symphony of peace, forevermore.
Each wave a whisper, a soothing refrain,
Cleansing the soul of sorrow and pain.

The salty breeze kisses the skin,
As the waves gently caress, drawing you in.
With each rhythmic pulse of the tide,
A sense of calm washes over, a feeling so wide.

Seagulls glide gracefully in the sky,
Their cries echoing, as they soar high.
The scent of salt and sea fills the air,
As the waves continue their rhythmic affair.

In the distance, the horizon meets the sky,
A seamless blend where dreams lie.
With each rise and fall of the tide,
The worries of the world seem to subside.

As the sun dips below the ocean's embrace,

Painting the sky with hues of grace,
The waves of serenity linger on,
A timeless melody, until the dawn.

For by the ocean's edge, where waves meet the shore,
A symphony of peace forevermore.
In the ebb and flow of the tide,
Find solace and serenity, side by side.

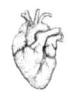

Footsteps in the Forest

Among the trees, where silence reigns,
Footsteps in the forest, leave their stains.
Each step a journey, through nature's grace,
In the forest's embrace, find your place.

Sunlight filters through the leafy canopy,
Casting shadows, both dark and free.
Birds chirp melodies, in harmonious tune,
Nature's symphony, beneath the moon.

Rustling leaves and gentle breeze,
Whisper secrets among the trees.
Moss-covered paths lead the way,
In the forest's heart, where spirits sway.

Creatures of the woods, both big and small,
Call this sanctuary their eternal hall.
Squirrels scurry, deer graze in peace,
In this woodland haven, worries cease.

In the stillness of the forest, find release,
In the quiet whisper of the trees.

Footsteps in the forest, echo through,
Guiding you on paths both old and new.

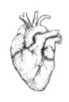

Whispers of Despair

In the silence of the night, where shadows creep,
Whispers of despair, dark secrets to keep.
Each breath a burden, each sigh a cry,
In the depths of darkness, lost souls lie.

Within the soul's labyrinth, where demons roam,
Whispers of despair, find their home.
Each whisper a torment, a relentless knell,
In the abyss of despair, where hope fell.

Beneath the veil of despair, where dreams decay,
Whispers of despair, hold sway.
Each whisper a reminder, of pain and woe,
In the depths of despair, where sorrows grow.

In the echoes of despair, where silence reigns,
Whispers of despair, leave their stains.
Each echo a lament, a cry for release,
In the realm of despair, where shadows cease.

Echoes of Regret

In the chambers of the heart, where memories dwell,
Echoes of regret, a haunting spell.
Each echo a reminder, of paths not taken,
In the labyrinth of the mind, hearts forsaken.

Within the recesses of the soul, where shadows hide,
Echoes of regret, silently bide.
Each echo a lament, for what could have been,
In the depths of regret, where dreams are unseen.

Beneath the weight of regret, where dreams lie shattered,
Echoes of regret, forever tattered.
Each echo a whisper, of chances missed,
In the realm of regret, where the heart persists.

In the echoes of regret, where silence reigns,
Echoes of regret, leave their stains.
Each echo a burden, too heavy to bear,
In the depths of regret, hearts lay bare.

Shadows of Sorrow

Beneath the cloak of night, where dreams decay,
Shadows of sorrow, in disarray.
Each shadow a specter, of pain and grief,
In the depths of despair, no solace, no relief.

Within the caverns of the mind, where fears reside,
Shadows of sorrow, they do confide.
Each shadow a reminder, of battles lost,
In the labyrinth of sorrow, hearts exhaust.

Underneath the veil of sorrow, where dreams fade,
Shadows of sorrow, in silent cascade.
Each shadow a memory, of love gone awry,
In the abyss of sorrow, souls cry.

In the shadows of sorrow, where silence reigns,
Shadows of sorrow, leave their stains.
Each shadow a burden, too heavy to bear,
In the depths of sorrow, hearts lay bare.

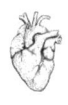

Dusk's Embrace

As twilight falls, casting shadows long,
Dusk's embrace, a melancholy song.
Each fading light, a whisper of the end,
In the fading twilight, darkness descends.

Within the twilight's grasp, where dreams take flight,
Dusk's embrace, a solace in the night.
Each moment fleeting, a sigh of release,
In the embrace of dusk, find peace.

Beneath the shroud of dusk, where shadows play,
Dusk's embrace, holds sway.
Each shadow a reminder, of the day's end,
In the twilight's grasp, souls blend.

In the dusk's embrace, where silence reigns,
Dusk's embrace, leaves its stains.
Each moment a fleeting, yet eternal grace,
In the depths of dusk, find solace, find grace.

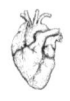

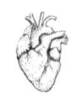

Whispers of the Void

In the emptiness of space, where stars grow dim,
Whispers of the void, a hollow hymn.
Each whisper a reminder, of insignificance,
In the vast expanse, a soul's repentance.

Within the void's depths, where darkness thrives,
Whispers of the void, where nothing survives.
Each whisper an echo, of lost hope,
In the void's grasp, souls elope.

In the depths of the void, where silence reigns,
Whispers of the void, leave their stains.
Each whisper a burden, too heavy to bear,
In the abyss of the void, souls despair.

Veil of Darkness

Underneath the veil of night, where demons lurk,
Veil of darkness, shadows smirk.
Each flicker a reminder, of sins untold,
In the veil of darkness, nightmares unfold.

Within the folds of darkness, where fears abide,
Veil of darkness, where shadows hide.
Each shadow a specter, of the night,
In the depths of darkness, no respite.

Beneath the shroud of darkness, where dreams decay,
Veil of darkness, in disarray.
Each shadow a torment, a relentless plight,
In the abyss of darkness, souls fight.

In the veil of darkness, where silence reigns,
Veil of darkness, leave their stains.
Each shadow a burden, too heavy to bear,
In the depths of darkness, hearts despair.

Echoes of Loss

In the halls of memory, where echoes dwell,
Echoes of loss, a mournful knell.
Each echo a lament, for what's been taken,
In the labyrinth of the mind, regrets parade.

Within the heart's chambers, where tears are shed,
Echoes of loss, where dreams are dead.
Each echo a reminder, of love once held dear,
In the depths of sorrow, hearts veer.

Beneath the weight of grief, where shadows lie,
Echoes of loss, silently cry.
Each echo a whisper, of souls departed,
In the realm of loss, the broken-hearted.

In the echoes of loss, where silence reigns,
Echoes of loss, leave their stains.
Each echo a burden, too heavy to bear,
In the depths of loss, souls lay bare.

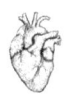

Break

In the quiet of the night,
Where dreams and darkness meet,
A heart once full of light,
Now echoes hollow beat.

Stars above seem cold and far,
Once so close, now stray.
Love's gentle kiss, a jagged scar,
Hope has lost its way.

Memories, bittersweet and pure,
Dance upon the breeze.
A love so strong, yet couldn't endure,
Brought to its tender knees.

Yet from the ashes, rise anew,
A heart that dares to mend.
For even in the deepest blue,
A broken heart can bend.

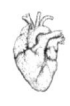

Shattered Soul

Among the ruins of the past,
A soul in fragments lies.
Each shard a story, cast
Into the endless skies.

The dreams once held so tight,
Now scattered in the wind.
The vibrant colors turned to night,
A tale that never sinned.

Yet in the pieces, there's a song,
A melody of might.
For even shattered, we belong
To the dance of endless light.

In every break, a strength concealed,
In every tear, a start.
A shattered soul can be revealed,
As a work of art.

Mistrust

In the eyes where once was faith,
A shadow now resides.
Trust, a fragile wraith,
In corners dark, it hides.

Whispers turn to echoed doubt,
Promises, mere ghosts.
Love, a realm where shadows flout,
And fear's the honored host.

Yet in the heart, a fire burns,
A beacon through the lies.
For trust, though broken, always yearns,
To rise, to realize.

In cautious steps, it finds its way,
Through mazes dark and wild.
And in the dawn of a new day,
The heart, once more, a child.

Hidden Pain

Behind the smile, the laughter bright,
A secret sorrow lives.
In the day, and in the night,
A pain that never gives.

Eyes that sparkle, voice so clear,
A mask so finely made.
Yet deep within, a well of tears,
In shadow, hearts do wade.

To bear a burden all alone,
To hide it from the light.
A strength, a courage, seldom shown,
In every silent fight.

Yet hope does bloom in quiet hours,
And comfort finds its place.
For even in the darkest towers,
Love's light will interlace.

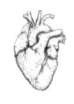

Teary Eyes

Teardrops fall like gentle rain,
From eyes that tell a tale.
A heart that knows the weight of pain,
Yet dreams will never fail.

Each tear a story, pure and clear,
Of joys and sorrows past.
Of moments held so dear,
Yet never meant to last.

In every drop, a universe,
In every fall, a grace.
For teary eyes, though they disperse,
Reflect a soul's embrace.

And when the tears have dried away,
A calm and peace remain.
For eyes that weep, and hearts that sway,
Know love will break the chain.

Lost Love

In the quiet dusk of time,
A love once bright has waned.
A melody without its rhyme,
A heart that's been refrained.

The memories, a bittersweet,
Of times when hearts did soar.
Now lost within the incomplete,
Where love is felt no more.

Yet in the echoes, faint and light,
A whisper still remains.
A promise of the endless night,
That love will heal the pains.

For even lost, love finds a way,
To linger, soft and true.
In every night, there's hope of day,
And love will break through.

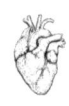

Silent Suffering

In the silence, shadows crawl,
A suffering unseen.
Behind closed doors, within the walls,
A heart's unheard, serene.

The pain is silent, yet it screams,
In whispers to the soul.
In haunted thoughts, and broken dreams,
Where shadows take their toll.

Yet in the quiet, strength does rise,
A power, fierce and bright.
For suffering that's in disguise,
Will find its voice in light.

And through the dark, and through the storm,
A spirit finds its flame.
In silent suffering, hearts transform,
And hope will speak its name.

Darkness Lies Heavy in the Heart

In the depths where shadows dwell,
A silence dark and stark,
There's a tale the heart won't tell,
Of a soul engulfed in dark.

Heavy lies the weight of night,
Upon a weary chest,
Stealing dreams and shrouding light,
In an endless, cold unrest.

Every beat a muted cry,
Every breath a sigh,
Hope, a distant, flickering light,
Lost within the sky.

Memories, like phantom streams,
Wander through the mind,
Casting doubts and breaking dreams,
Leaving peace behind.

Whispers of forgotten fears
Echo through the gloom,

Washing over eyes with tears,
In this melancholy room.

Lonely nights and restless days,
Merge into one gray blur,
In a maze of sorrowed haze,
Where heart and darkness stir.

Stars once bright now faintly gleam,
Beneath the heavy veil,
Longing for the lost daydream,
In a night that seems to wail.

Each moment, a silent scream,
In the cavern of the soul,
Lost within a mournful dream,
Where shadows take their toll.

Yet in the heart, a flicker glows,
A spark that won't depart,
For even in the deepest woes,
Light lingers in the heart.

Though darkness heavy lies within,
And shadows cloud the way,
A heart that beats will rise again,
To greet the break of day.

Through the thickest, darkest night,
Through despair's tight grip,
There shines a beacon, pure and bright,
A hope that will not slip.

For hearts are stronger than they seem,
And souls can brave the dark,
In every shadow, there's a beam,
A hidden, hopeful spark.

So carry on through endless shade,
Through trials hard and stark,
For in the end, the night will fade,
And dawn will find the heart.

About the Author

Joshua Pavelsky, born in the small town of Picayune, Mississippi, is a unique individual with a passion for storytelling, culinary arts, and digital adventures. As a writer, he draws inspiration from literary greats like Edgar Allan Poe and personal heroes such as his grandfather. A graduate from Wilson, North Carolina, Joshua has ventured into various fields, establishing himself as an entrepreneur and a devoted father who cherishes every moment with his child. In addition to his literary pursuits, Joshua is an avid car and motorcycle enthusiast with a keen interest in racing. When he's not writing or spending time with his family, he can often be found honing his skills in the kitchen or immersed in the latest video games. Joshua's diverse interests and experiences bring a unique perspective to his work, captivating readers with his imaginative poetry. and deep appreciation for the finer details of life.

About the Publisher

Fae Corps is all about helping the Indie Author find the magic in their art. We are the authors and the small storytellers. We are all about helping the new and struggling authors to be seen. We are all about helping the indie author to find their voice. We believe in the indie author's magic to make a difference in this world.

Find us at faecorpspublishing.org and our catalog is available at Books2read.com/rl/faecorpsllc

Milton Keynes UK
Ingram Content Group UK Ltd.
UKHW021628090824
446663UK00019B/437